Copyright © 2013 by Ra'Shin T. Akins

All rights reserved

Printed in the United States of America

International Standard Book Number: 978-0615806532

GGKM Publishing

P.O. Box 6032

Warner Robins, GA 31095-6032

(478) 919-4128

This book or parts thereof may not be reproduced in any form without prior written permission of the publisher

Unless otherwise noted, all Scripture quotations are from the Holy Bible, King James Version.

First printing, January 2001

Second printing, May 2002

Hebrew and Greek definitions are taken from Strong's Concordance.

Copyright © 1995, 1996, Thomas Nelson Publishers

Dedication

This book is the first fruit of many. Therefore, I dedicate this book to the Father, GOD Himself. As Abraham was willing to offer Isaac, the promised seed, so I offer this achievement unto Him. As Hannah gave her promise Samuel back to the Lord, so I give this first fruit back to the One that gave it to me to birth. Without You Father, this would not have been possible. I am nothing without You Lord. Thank You for investing all that You have in me.

And my prayer is that You continue to lead and guide me to the place that You have predestined for my life. I ask that You accept this first fruit of a plentiful harvest. I stand on Your Word and I hold fast to the promises that You have spoken over my life. And I receive them in the name of Your son Jesus Christ. Thank You Father for all you have done.

Acknowledgements

My deepest appreciation to:

My beautiful wife, Donna - Our journey together has helped produced this baby. Through the good and the bad, I've loved you continually. Words cannot explain how much you mean to me. So I will continually try my best to explain it through my actions. And, by faith, I believe that the sky is the limit for us. The best is yet to come. I LOVE YOU LADY A.

My children, Dominique, RaShay, Marc-Quan, Anthony, Jasmine, Enigue, Tyanna, and Ra'Shin II - I pray that this book will be an example to you that shows that you can accomplish anything that you set your mind to do. Set your goals and achieve them. And always remember to put GOD first. I love you.

My mother, Lisa Akins-Parker – When everyone counted me out, you continued to see the greatness in your son. You believed in me when all the evidence said it was a waste of time to do so. Thank you for a mother's love that transcends all of my mistakes. And I pray that all three of my daughters have inherited your strength. I love you mommy.

To my father, Thomas E. Douglas Sr., and step-father, Leonardo J. Parker – Your combined wisdom and work ethic has inspired me to push pass my circumstances and make something out of nothing. I want you both to know that when it appeared that I wasn't listening, I heard loud and clear. Your labor was not in vain. Thank you for all that you have done. I love you.

To my siblings, Shawn, Vashti, Teresa, Thomas Jr., Gideon, Sharron, and Latoya - One could not ask for a better set of brothers and sisters. Thank you for all of your support. I love you all.

To my grandmother, Sallie, and great grandmother, Fannie - You two have passed down priceless treasures of wisdom, values, and heritage. I am blessed to have two strong and resilient women that I can draw from when I need guidance. I see where my mother gets it from. I love you ladies.

To the Akins family - To all my aunts, uncles, cousins, nieces and nephews. I love you all greatly. And I am proud to share the Akins name with you.

To two special Akins family members, my spiritual father and mother, Apostle Daniel L. Akins and Pastor Vonyett Akins – Words can't express the appreciation and gratitude that I have. You have allowed GOD to use you to groom my wife and I into the man and woman of GOD that we are today. I am forever grateful for your sacrifices and the love that you have shown us beyond that of a blood relative . I love you both dearly.

To the RGMI family – Thank you for all of your support. For the love that you've all shown my family and I. Thank you for all that you do. I love you.

Contents

Introduction 13

1. The Natural Peasant 16

2. The Mental Peasant 21

3. The Spiritual Peasant 25

4. Overcoming Rejection and the Spirit of Rejection 30

5. Patience vs. Frustration 39

6. Time vs. Season 47

7. Working Under The Pressure 57

8.	Enoch vs. Enoch	67
9.	Don't Settle for the Vial, Wait on the Horn	81
10.	Awake	99
11.	You Are Closer Than You Think	106
12.	All Hail the King	112

Introduction

Greatness: The quality of being great, distinguished, or eminent. It is a quality that lives on the inside of every child of GOD. Though the areas of greatness differ, there is a seed of it in every believer waiting to be birthed. The problem that a lot of Christians face is that we are not aware of or not able to tap into the greatness that is dwelling within so that we can be the King, or the Queen, that we truly are. Because of this, we are forced to live beneath our privileges. We are forced to live like peasants when, in fact, we are royalty.

1Peter 2:9
But ye are a chosen generation, a royal priesthood, an holy nation, a peculiar people; that ye should shew forth the praises of him who hath called you out of darkness into his marvelous light:

A peasant is a poor farmer of low social status. Not only is this a natural issue, it is also a mental and a spiritual issue. One leads to the other causing a chain reaction of things that lead to the confining of the believer's inner King.

In this book, The KING Inside The Peasant, my goal (with the leading of the Holy Spirit) is to reveal to the believer exactly who and WHO is living on the inside of them. There is a tag team present just waiting to be activated. By tag team I mean the first who which is the Great you, and the ultimate WHO which is JESUS CHRIST. In the upcoming chapters, a light will be shined on the issues of the peasant and what makes he or she the way that they are. Once this knowledge has been revealed, then the keys of solution will be given to unlock the doors which holds you, the King or Queen, hostage.

Chapter 1
The Natural Peasant

In a **natural** sense, the believer has to endure the present reality where he or she does not have finances, resources, respect, and acceptance. They are least esteemed among peers that appear to be prosperous. And their input is not welcomed.

Ecclesiastes 9:16
Then said I, wisdom is better than strength: nevertheless the poor man's wisdom is despised, and his words are not heard.

I've learned through experience that if a person is not at a certain status, then whatever he or she says or thinks has no impact. Not because it is not true, sound, wise, or just the right thing to do, but it is in fact the packaging that the gift is wrapped in that poses the problem. People are not receptive to advice or help from those whom they <u>feel</u> are beneath them. Even if, through the peasant, GOD has given the answers that they desperately need. They would rather drink from a shallow pond rather than a deep well.

Jeremiah 2:13
For my people have committed two evils; they have <u>forsaken me</u> the fountain of living waters, and hewed them out cisterns, broken cisterns, that can hold no water.

And they are satisfied with this as long as they don't have to accredit the peasant for his or her input. For better understanding, let's use the example of King Saul and David.

1Samuel 18:10-11
10 And it came to pass on the morrow, that the evil <u>***spirit***</u> ***from God came upon Saul, and he prophesied in the midst of the house: and David played with his hand, as at other times: and there was a javelin in Saul's hand.***

11 And Saul cast the javelin; for he said, I will smite David even to the wall with it. And David avoided out of his presence twice.

Prior to this incident, in 1Samuel 15:26, Saul has been rejected by GOD for disobedience. Because of this, GOD took the kingdom from Saul and gave it to another, a peasant shepherd boy by the name of David. To the natural eye, it would appear that Saul would remain king for many years after. But in GOD's eyesight, David was the man. David's popularity grew among the people because of his abilities and anointing. But it was Saul that could see the KING in David and it drove him to jealousy and envy. Which brings us back to 1 Samuel 18:10-11, David had the ability to drive an evil spirit away from Saul by his skillful playing of the harp. But instead of seeing David as a blessing, Saul could not put his pride aside.

Instead, he chose to throw a javelin at David. David's help was not wanted because of <u>who</u> was inside of him.

Peasants will always have javelins thrown at them in ordered to kill the inner king and keep him from surfacing. This could pose to be frustrating when the peasant is gifted, talented, and anointed but cannot seem to bridge the gap between poverty (both natural and spiritual) and success. This leaves the peasant believer with the impression that he or she is worthless. Thus the natural dilemma leads to a mental dilemma.

Chapter 2
<u>The Mental Peasant</u>

The mental peasant is led by the present circumstances that they are faced with. Their natural poverty causes them to be poor in their thinking. Because of their current storms, they mentally don't see themselves past their present situation. They sink into a thought pattern that says, "This is how I'm supposed to be". This is far from the truth. But until the peasant is made aware of their true identity, **AND BELIEVES IT**, then they will remain in an impoverished state. He or she must overcome this way of thinking and unlock the vault of riches in their mind which causes them to dream. And they must envision themselves in their wealthy place.

Psalms 66:12
Thou hast caused men to ride over our heads; we went though fire and through water: but thou broughtest us out into a wealthy place.

It is Satan's desire to magnify a natural situation so that he may have you bound in your mind. This is because he knows that if any change or progress is going to take place, it will start there. He also knows that if he can continue to manipulate the believer's thoughts, then change will never occur. Therefore, it is very important for the mind of the peasant to be continually renewed.

Romans 12:2
And be not conformed to the things of this world: but be ye transformed by the renewing of your mind, that ye may prove what is that good and acceptable, and perfect, will of God.

The peasant must always remember that it is GOD's desire that he or she is successful.

3 John vs. 2
Beloved, I wish above all things that thou mayest prosper and be in health, even as thy soul prosper.

With that said, the peasant must do whatever it takes to protect their minds from the psychological attacks of Satan.

1Peter 1:13
Wherefore gird up the loins of your mind, be sober, and hope to the end for the grace that is to be brought unto you at the revelation of Jesus Christ.

If the believer can do this, then he or she is well on their way to being crowned. If not, then the peasant's mental dilemma graduates into a spiritual dilemma.

Chapter 3
<u>The Spiritual Peasant</u>
"Them of little faith"

The Spiritual peasant is the most dangerous. He or she looks at their natural situation, becomes mentally bound, and then creates more natural and mental problems by speaking death into their situation. They release the spirit of doubt, unbelief, depression, and various other negative spirits to contend with. And they bring more warfare upon themselves.

Proverbs 18:21
<u>Death and life are</u> in the power of the tongue: and they that love it shall eat the fruit thereof.

The peasant has the ability to change his/her circumstances with just a positive word. But because of the peasant mentality that they live in, they believe what they see and speak more negativity into the atmosphere. This does not allow their spiritual muscle, which is **_Faith_** to be exercised. And when faith is not properly exercised, like any muscle, it gets weak. Since **GOD** is moved by our faith, it is important that we walk strong in it. How do we do that you say? I'm glad you asked. We do that by trusting in **GOD** regardless of any circumstance or situation. Any problem that we face should not overshadow the Words that **GOD** has spoken unto us. **GOD** has the last say so, not our problems.   The bible says in

2 Corinthians 5:7
(For we walk by faith, not by sight:)

The peasant may not naturally or mentally see the King/Queen inside of them, but by **_Faith_**, they must believe that he/she is there. Our faith tells **GOD** that we believe that we are who **HE** says that we are. Not what others or sometimes even we ourselves say that we are. The patriarch Abraham is a perfect example of how to exercise faith in what seems to be an impossible situation.

Romans 4:18&19

18 Who against hope <u>believed in hope</u>, that he might become the father of many nations, according to that which was spoken, So shall thy seed be.

19 And being <u>not weak in faith</u>, he considered not his own body now dead, when he was about an hundred years old, neither yet the deadness of Sarah's womb:

Hebrews 11:8&9
8 <u>By faith</u> Abraham, when he was called to go out into a place which he should after receive for an inheritance, <u>obeyed</u>; and he went out, not knowing whither he went.

9 <u>By faith</u> he <u>sojourned</u> in the land of promise, as in a strange *country, dwelling in tabernacles with Isaac and Jacob, the heirs with him of the same promise*

We believe what **GOD** says and **GOD**, in **HIS** timing, will perform it.

Hebrews 11:6
<u>But without faith</u> it is impossible to please him: for he that cometh to God <u>must believe that he is,</u> and that he is a rewarder of them diligently seek him.

Chapter 4
<u>Overcoming Rejection and the Spirit of Rejection</u>

Now that we have exposed the problems that the peasant faces, let us now work toward delivering him/her from them. One of the most important ways to do so is overcoming rejection and a spirit of rejection. One is different from the other but both can stop the peasant's forward progress into royalty.

<u>Rejection</u>

Rejection is simply the act of rejecting something or a state of being rejected. If not careful, this enemy can cripple the peasant because it will have he/she starving for acceptance from negative sources. And when a person is in this state, it is easy for them to compromise key values in order to fit in. For example, a person that does not smoke lights up a cigarette because everyone that they think is cool is doing it. And for fear of not appearing cool, they compromise their own personal beliefs to appease those that they idolize and put on pedestals. Instead of standing up for what he/she believes is right, this person takes the easy road hoping to gain the attention that they so crave. But instead, he/she becomes slaves to negative influences. And instead of gaining the respect and popularity he/she desires, this person must continue to lower themselves beneath what they know is right to continue to maintain this false sense of acceptance. The peasant must be aware of and understand that rejection comes with the territory.

Again, David, a man after **GOD**'s own heart suffered rejection in many areas. Even from his own family. When the prophet Samuel came to anoint Israel's new king among Jesse's sons, David was not even called by his father to be considered.

I Samuel 16:6-10
6 And it came to pass, when they were come, that he looked on Eliab, and said, Surely the LORD'S anointed is before him.

7 But <u>the LORD said</u> unto Samuel, Look not on his countenance, or on the height of his stature; because I have refused him: for the LORD seeth not as man seeth; for man <u>looketh on</u> the outward appearance, but <u>the LORD looketh on</u> the heart.

8 Then Jesse called Abinadab, and made him pass before Samuel, And he said, Neither hath the LORD chosen this.

9 Then Jesse made Shammah to pass by. And he said, Neither hath the LORD chosen this.

10 Again, Jesse made seven of his sons to pass before Samuel. And

Samuel said unto Jesse, The LORD hath not chosen these.

It can be devastating when you are rejected by those close to you. Those that you feel you should have the most support from. But even though man overlooks you, **GOD** knows exactly where you are.

I Samuel 16:11
And Samuel said unto Jesse, Are here all thy children? And he said, There remaineth yet the youngest, and behold, he keepeth the sheep. And Samuel said unto Jesse, Send and fetch him: for we will not sit down till he come hither.

Satan knows who you really are

and is continually trying to stop you from becoming what you are destined to be. If the peasant can understand that, then he/she can survive the hurt and disappointment that comes with rejection. If not, then the peasant can become bound by a spirit of rejection.

<u>The spirit of rejection</u>
The spirit of rejection is a demon spirit that enters in through rejection that has not been overcome. It attaches itself to it's victim and has the victim believing that EVERYONE is against them. They perceive everything negatively. They resist help, sound advice, and wisdom by labeling it as an attack against them. They feel no one

understands them. The spirit of rejection leads them to believe that they have to isolate themselves from the rest of the world because they are right and everyone else is wrong. They have a belief that," I am in this by myself". Even some preachers and leaders fall victim to this spirit. They are not accepted in certain circles so they develop a way of thinking that tells them that they have elevated to a certain place or level in **GOD**. And that the reason that they are being rejected is that the people rejecting them have not yet reached that level. So to make themselves feel better about being rejected, they recreate themselves into some great person. But THIS great person is not the true great being that lives within them. It is true that when you live for **GOD** and strive to be more like **Jesus Christ,** you will be met with rejection from the world. But when you allow the spirit of rejection to deceive you to the point where you believe that your friends are your foes, then you can never make any steps forward. **BUT THERE IS HOPE!!!** Through much prayer, fasting, and determination, the peasant can be delivered from this spirit and any other demonic spirits.

Matthew 17:21
Howbeit this kind goeth not out but by <u>prayer and fasting.</u>

And after he/she is delivered, then rejection will no longer be a hindrance. But it will be a tool to push the peasant toward his/her destiny.

Chapter 5
Patience vs Frustration

The bible says in

Romans 5:3
And not only so, but we glory in tribulations also: knowing that tribulation worketh patience;

On our road to greatness, we experience various trials and much tribulation. We are attacked in many different ways in many different areas. **GOD** allows this because **He** wants to build patience in us.

Patience: the capacity to accept or tolerate delay, trouble, or suffering without getting angry or upset.

It is simply endurance. Patience is not easy to master. **GOD** leads us through certain trials and tribulations in order to pull out of us this precious gem. Without patience, we can never completely transform into the king/queen that **GOD** desires for us to be. So it is very important that in every test we acquire more patience. But we must be relentless in doing so because, as I mentioned before, gaining patience is sometimes easier said than done. We must also be mindful that, though **GOD** desires more patience out of your tests, Satan also expects something out of what you are going through. But what he wants to see out of you is frustration, not patience.

Frustration: the feeling of being upset or annoyed, especially because of inability to change or achieve something.

As you may have already noticed, frustration is the total opposite of patience. Satan wants us to grow weary in waiting on **GOD**'s promises to materialize in our lives. He wants us to focus more on the timing and not the season. (More explanation on timing and season will be given in the next chapter.) Satan's main desire is to cause us to get upset because we don't see the results that **we** want to see, when we want to see them. This is what happened to Abraham and Sarah. (Genesis16:1) Sarah got impatient with **GOD**'s promise that she would birth a son. Because of this, she urged her HUSBAND Abraham to sleep with her handmaid, Hagar. Hagar became pregnant and, after much tension between her and Sarah, birthed a son by the name of Ishmael. But he was not the son of **GOD**'s promise. In fact, in Genesis 21, when **GOD** did fulfill **HIS** promise and Sarah birthed their son Isaac, Hagar's son Ishmael began to mock Isaac. How many times have we birthed something, through impatience, that mocks our promise today? Satan wants us to lose hope and become frustrated because of the process that it takes to go from peasant to royalty. But we must never lose hope.

Romans 8:25
But if we hope for that we see not, then do we <u>with patience</u> wait for it.

Patience is key in this walk. Remember, a peasant is a poor **farmer** of low social status. And any good farmer is a patient one. A good farmer understands that when he/she plants a seed, the ground must first be cultivated. Then, after the seed is planted, the farmer must water it and give it sunlight. This is the easy part. The hard part is the most time consuming part of the whole process. The farmer must **WAIT**. If not careful, the wait can be frustrating because a seed grows down in the earth to get rooted before it grows up out of the ground. The peasant is the same. Things tend to seem worse before they get better. But none the less, through all of this, the peasant is growing into that king/queen. The seed must first get rooted and grounded to gain stability. And while waiting, the farmer must prevent pests and weeds from destroying their seed. For their harvest is in the seed. An unwise farmer will use steroids in order to speed up the process. But though the fruit will look of age, it will not reach it's full potential. It will be bitter and not perform in the way it was meant to. We must patiently protect the seed which is the king/queen inside us until it is time to be harvested. And not use spiritual steroids in an attempt to be crowned before our time. For if we do this, we bypass process. Not gaining certain tools, knowledge, and wisdom that we will need to reign correctly and effectively. We strive unlawfully or cheat, if you will, to grasp a prize which is already ours if we do it the right way and wait patiently on our <u>appointed</u> time.

2Timothy 2:5
And <u>if</u> a man also strive for masteries, yet is he not crowned, <u>except</u> he strive lawfully.

Job 14:14
If a man die, shall he live again? All the days of my appointed time will I wait, till my change come.

Therefore, be patient and not frustrated so that we may obtain everything that **GOD** wants to give us in order to be the king/queen that **HE** wants us to be.

James 1:4
<u>But let</u> patience have her perfect work, <u>that</u> ye may be perfect and entire, wanting nothing.

Chapter 6
Time vs Season

Ecclesiastes 3:1-8
1 To every thing there is a season, and a time to every purpose under the heaven:

2 A time to be born, and a time to die; a time to plant, and a time to pluck up that which is planted;

3 A time to kill, and a time to heal; a time to break down, and a time to build up;

4 A time to weep, and time to laugh; a time to mourn, and a time to dance;

5 A time to cast away stones, and a time to gather stones together; a time to embrace, and a time to refrain from embracing;

6 A time to get, and a time to lose; a time to keep, and a time to cast away;

7 A time to rend, and a time to sew; a time to keep silence, and a **time** *to speak;*

8 A time to love, and a time to hate; a time of war, and a time of peace;

No king/queen is on the exact same schedule. Some may seem to blossom faster than others. What discourages the peasant is not knowing the difference between time and season.

Time: (v) Plan, schedule, or arrange when(something) should happen or be done:

We sometimes get discouraged because we set our own time and schedules as to when WE think things should happen for us. But **GOD**'s planning is different and will often interrupt or cancel ours. HIS plans for us are far greater than the plans we have set for ourselves. And the road HE leads us on is very different from the path we want to take.

Isaiah 55:8
For my thoughts are not your thoughts, neither are your ways my ways, saith the LORD.

Human nature has us always seeking a quick and easy way to accomplish everything. We'd rather use the microwave of life rather than the oven. The microwave gives us what we want fast. But it lessons the quality. However the oven takes longer. But the more time and detail that is given, the better the quality. You must first be prepared by various ingredients in order to go in the oven. And once put in, you must endure the fire for a designated period of time. You are checked on periodically to see if you are done and to make sure that no harm comes to you. And if not done, back in the fire you go. But don't worry. The baker (**GOD**) will not let you overcook or burn. Correct process does not just happen. It takes time and effort. Take, for instance, the potter and the clay. Clay is a very fined-grained soil that is plastic when moist but hard when fired. When moist, the clay is corruptible. It can be shaped into anything the potter desires. But the potter must stretch it, bend it, and twist it in the way that it should go. This is not always easy because moist clay is not always willing to cooperate. We are like clay when **GOD** wants to mold us into a king or a queen. We are not always willing to let **GOD** mold us right. And we allow ourselves to be corrupted, marred, and shaped contrary to **GOD**'s perfect design for us. We are not stable and when we are put into the oven (a fiery trial) we cannot bare it and we fall apart or come out undone and deformed. As a result the potter, (**GOD**), cannot use us in the way that **HE** had intended. And we are no good to anyone or even ourselves. It is then that we must allow the potter, (**GOD**), to reshape us. And this time allow **HIM** to finish the job, no matter how long it takes. And once we emerge, we will be equipped with everything we need. We will be hard and tough, a strong king/queen.

Jeremiah 18:1-6
1 The word which came to Jeremiah from the LORD, saying,

2 Arise, and go down to the potter's house, and there I will cause thee to hear my words.

3 Then I went down to the potter's house, and, behold he wrought a work on the wheels. 4 And the vessel that he made of clay was marred in the hand of the potter: so he made it again another vessel, as seemed good to the potter to make it.

5 Then the word of the LORD came to me, saying,

6 O house of Israel, cannot I do with you as this potter? saith the LORD. Behold, as the clay is In the potter's hand, so are ye in mine hand, O house of Israel.

We disappoint ourselves when <u>we</u> decide how we should excel.

Usually, those are the times when we go through the most important processes. And we often forfeit the benefits we were to gain during them because we looked to gain something different. It was a time to gain spiritually but we looked for natural gain. It is important that the peasant manages his time wisely. And seek out GOD's desire for his/her life. It is only then that they can acquire every blessing in their totality.

Matthew 6:33
But seek ye <u>first</u> the kingdom of God, and his righteousness; and <u>all these things</u> shall be added unto you.

Once you have met **GOD**'s schedule, there is a designated season with your name on it.

Season: a suitable or natural time or occasion

When it is your season, there is nothing that Satan can do to stop it, though he will try. You have used your time wisely, let GOD mold you, and you've endured every test. You have been tried by fire and came out as pure gold. Your season is a harvest of all the seeds that you have sown. It is the result of your labor and patience. You've allowed yourself to suffer with Christ. And now it is time to reign with him.

2Timothy 2:2

If we suffer, we shall reign with him: if we deny him, he also will deny us:

Chapter 7
Working Under the Pressure

During the processing that we go through to reach our destiny, we often have a strong desire to give up and quit. The pressures that we encounter, at times, seem extremely overwhelming. We say to ourselves and even to **GOD**, "This is too much", "I can't take this anymore", "Why would a GOD that is supposed to love me let me go through this", "I just don't believe that **GOD** wants me here". Any of these sound familiar? We all, at some point in time, experience these feelings. This is normal for any human being. BUT, we cannot stay there too long. We must learn to fight through these feelings and keep moving forward. Sometimes we have to encourage ourselves and tell ourselves that we are right where **GOD** wants us. And if we are still not sure, ask **HIM** for direction.

1Samuel 30:6-8
6 And David was greatly distressed; for the people spake of stoning him, because the soul of all the people was grieved, every man for his sons and for his daughters: <u>but David encouraged himself in the Lord his God.</u>

7 And David said to Abiathar the priest, Ahimelech's son, I pray thee, bring me hither the ephod.

And Abiathar brought thither the ephod to David.

*8 **And David enquired at the Lord**, saying, Shall I pursue after this troop? shall I overtake them? And he answered him, Pursue: for thou shalt surely overtake them, and without fail recover all.*

Proverbs 3:6
6 **In all thy ways acknowledge him, and he shall direct thy paths.**

GOD will always give you the direction that you need. But that does not mean that the pressure will go away or even lighten up.

2 Timothy 2:3
3 Thou therefore endure

hardness, as a good soldier of Jesus Christ.

This simply means to fight through the pressure and complete the assignment that **GOD** has charged you to complete. The pressure that you are experiencing now is just preparing you for something greater. NOTHING that **GOD** does is by accident. **HE** knows exactly what **HE** wants you to do and where **HE** wants you to do it. And **HE** knows, ahead of time, the challenges you will face. And **HE** also knows that **HE** has already well equipped you for the task at hand. When I think of this, I think of a man called Gideon.

Judges 6:11

11 And there came an angel of the Lord, and sat under an oak which was in Ophrah, that pertained unto Joash the Abiezrite: and his son Gideon threshed wheat by the winepress, to hide it from the Midianites.

Here Gideon is working. He is threshing wheat. This symbolizes separation. Wheat must be separated from tare because the seeds of the tare are poisonous. And by staying connected to the wheat, it can infect the wheat and kill it. The key is, knowing the difference between the two. Wheat and tare look similar and the only way to separate them is to beat the two on the threshing floor and then toss both in the air. The wind will carry the tare away while the wheat will remain. In order to become a true king or queen, we must at times learn how to separate ourselves from people and things that will poison us. Sometimes, in order to do so, we must be beat or experience pressure. What I like about Gideon is that he was working by the winepress. Threshing wheat was supposed to be done at a designated place. And at the designated place, it would have been easier and more convenient for Gideon to do the job. But because of the pressure he was under, (fear of losing what was valuable to him), he was forced to work by a winepress. Gideon was at a place that was **designed** to apply pressure. A winepress exerts controlled pressure in order to free the juice from the grape. The pressure must be controlled, especially with grapes, in order to avoid crushing the seeds and releasing a great deal of undesirable tannins into the wine. Symbolically, Gideon was working at a place designed to apply just enough pressure to squeeze the very best out of you and I so that others that thirst may drink from us. The pressure is not in vain. **GOD** is trying to get the best out of us through every trial and test in order to one day help bring another king or queen out of their shell. And **HE** knows just how much pressure each of us needs to bring the wine out of us without killing the seeds in us which will one day birth **HIS** desire in the earth. And without releasing tannins which would cause us to be bitter and dry up. Gideon, because he was pressed, went on to do great things in the kingdom. But Gideon himself battled challenges of a peasant. Gideon's name means to hide, to cause to flee. But when **GOD** approached him, **HE** called him a mighty man of valour and that **HE** had sent Gideon to accomplished what seemed to be impossible. Gideon felt inadequate because his family was poor and that he was the least in his father's house. He had concerns because of what was going on around him. And it seemed like GOD was not with Israel. But **GOD**, knowing all of this already, said that **HE** would be with him. Sometimes we can be in despair because of what is happening all around us and not even realize that **GOD** is grooming **us** to be the deliverer that we were seeking.

Judges 6:12-16
12 And the angel of the Lord appeared unto him, and said unto him, The Lord is with thee, thou mighty man of valour.

13 And Gideon said unto him, Oh my Lord, if the Lord be with us, why then is all this befallen us? and where be all his miracles which our fathers told us of, saying, Did not the Lord bring us up from Egypt? but now the Lord hath forsaken us, and delivered us into the hands of the Midianites.

14 And the Lord looked upon him, and said, Go in this thy might, and thou shalt save Israel from the hand of the Midianites: have not I sent thee?

15 And he said unto him, Oh my Lord, wherewith shall I save Israel? behold, my family is poor in Manasseh, and I am the least in my father's house.

16 And the Lord said unto him, Surely I will be with thee, and thou shalt smite the Midianites as one man.

Pressure is placed in our lives to perfect us. The more we can work through it and under it, the greater the king/queen we will become.

Chapter 8
<u>Enoch vs. Enoch</u>

The bible speaks of **two** men by the name of Enoch. The Enoch born unto Cain, and the Enoch in the lineage of Seth. They both have the same name but they differ in agenda. They represent two different types of believer. In researching the meaning of the name, the name actually has two different spellings, in Hebrew, and two different definitions. One Hebrew spelling and definition is :

Chanaq - To choke oneself to death (by a rope), hang self, strangle.

(Refer to The New Strong's Exhaustive Concordance of the Bible)

Let's deal first with Chanaq. He represents the Enoch that is born unto Cain.
This Enoch is the son of the first murderer that the bible records. He is the seed of him that slew his brother Abel. Both were the sons of the first man, Adam, and his wife Eve.

Genesis 4:1-2
1 And Adam knew Eve his wife; and she conceived, and bare Cain, and said, I have gotten a man from the Lord.

2 And she again bare his brother Abel. And Abel was a keeper of sheep, but Cain was a tiller of the ground.

Cain slew Abel because Abel presented an acceptable offering unto **GOD**. And the **LORD** respected Abel's offering but did not respect Cain's.

Genesis 4:3-8
3 And in process of time it came to pass, that Cain brought of the fruit of the ground an offering unto the Lord.

4 And Abel, he also brought of the firstlings of his flock and of the fat thereof. And the Lord had respect unto Abel and to his offering:

5 But unto Cain and to his offering he had not respect. And Cain was very wroth, and his countenance fell.

6 And the Lord said unto Cain, Why art thou wroth? and why is thy countenance fallen?

7 If thou doest well, shalt thou not be accepted? and if thou doest not well, sin lieth at the door. And unto thee shall be his desire, and thou shalt rule over him.

8 And Cain talked with Abel his brother: and it came to pass, when they were in the field, that Cain rose up against Abel his brother, and slew him.

Cain refused to do what was

pleasing in the sight of the **LORD**, even when **GOD** gave him another opportunity. Instead his actions caused the death of his brother. And now he has passed his murderess tendencies to his son Enoch. Remember, Chanaq means to choke oneself to death (by a rope), hang self, strangle. You will always kill your inner king or queen when you do not seek to please **GOD** and do what is acceptable in **HIS** sight. Cain's type of offering did not change even after Abel's death. When Enoch was born, instead of honoring **GOD** with a proper offering, he honored Enoch instead. He built a city and named it after Enoch.

Genesis 4:17

17 And Cain knew his wife; and she conceived, and bare Enoch: and he builded a city, and called the name of the city, after the name of his son, Enoch.

Cain made no mention of the **LORD** his **GOD** but only his son of whom, by the way, the **LORD** gave him. It is dangerous, when trying to become great, to ignore **HIM** who is to crown us. The peasant should never put anything or anyone before **GOD**, making little gods and idols that will hinder his/her coronation. This type of Enoch will always have cities built after his own name and not the name of the **LORD**. We should not walk after this example. This example will not allow our inner royalty to emerge.

The peasant should always seek to please **GOD** by focusing on building **HIS** kingdom. And by doing so, reap the benefits of **HIS** kingdom.

Matthew 6:33
33But seek you first the kingdom of God, and his righteousness; and all these things shall be added unto you.

The other Hebrew spelling and definition is:

Chanak – To initiate or discipline, dedicate, or train up.
(Refer to The New Strong's Exhaustive Concordance of the Bible)

This is the Enoch in the lineage of

Seth.

Genesis 4:25
25 And Adam knew his wife again; and she bare a son, and called his name Seth: For God, said she, hath appointed me another seed instead of Abel, whom Cain slew.

Seth's name , in the Hebrew tongue, is Sheth and it means substituted.
(Refer to The New Strong's Exhaustive Concordance of the Bible)

GOD gave Seth to Adam and Eve as a substitute for Abel, the son whom Cain slew. Because of Cain's refusal to present the correct offering, **GOD** had to raise up a replacement for Abel, one that will be acceptable in **HIS** sight. One that is disciplined and dedicated. One that will not only call upon the name of the **LORD**, but will train up his children to call upon the name of the **LORD** as well.

Genesis 4:26
26 And to Seth, to him also there was born a son; and he called his name Enos: then began men to call upon the name of the Lord.

Proverbs 22:6
Train up a child in the way he should go: and when he is old, he will not depart from it.

Through the seed of Seth came this second Enoch of whose

example we <u>should</u> follow.

Genesis 5:6-22
6 And Seth lived an hundred and five years, and begat Enos:

7 And Seth lived after he begat Enos eight hundred and seven years, and begat sons and daughters:

8 And all the days of Seth were nine hundred and twelve years: and he died.

9 And Enos lived ninety years, and begat Cainan:

10 And Enos lived after he begat Cainan eight hundred and fifteen years, and begat sons and daughters:

11 And all the days of Enos were nine hundred and five years: and he died.

12 And Cainan lived seventy years and begat Mahalaleel:

13 And Cainan lived after he begat Mahalaleel eight hundred and forty years, and begat sons and daughters:

14 And all the days of Cainan were nine hundred and ten years: and he died.

15 And Mahalaleel lived sixty and five years, and begat Jared:

16 And Mahalaleel lived after he begat Jared eight hundred and thirty years, and begat sons and daughters:

17 And all the days of Mahalaleel were eight hundred ninety and five years: and he died.

18 And Jared lived an hundred sixty and two years, and he begat Enoch:

19 And Jared lived after he begat Enoch eight hundred years, and begat sons and daughters:

20 And all the days of Jared were nine hundred sixty and two years: and he died.

21 And Enoch lived sixty and five years, and begat Methuselah:

22 And Enoch walked with God after he begat Methuselah three hundred years, and begat sons and daughters:

The bible says that **this** Enoch, whose name means to initiate, discipline, dedicate, or train up, walked with **GOD**. If the peasant is going to ever be anything great, then he or she must learn how to walk with **GOD**. We must be a co-laborer with **HIM**.

1 Corinthians 3:9
9For we are labourers together with God: ye are God's husbandry, ye are God's building.

GOD will not just bring the king or queen out of us. We must work together with **HIM** in order see it.

Genesis 5:24
24 And Enoch walked with God: and he was not; for God took him.

This Enoch's walk with **GOD** was so intimate, that he did not see death. **GOD** simply took him. And if we as peasants ever want to experience the LIFE that **GOD** promised us, then it is essential that we learn how to walk with **HIM**. Though at times it may seem difficult, if we can master this as Enoch (Chanak) did, then and only then will GOD do what he did for Enoch. HE will take us places.

Chapter 9
<u>Don't Settle For The Vial, Wait On The Horn</u>

There are two ways that a king can be anointed. They are the anointing of the vial of oil and the anointing of the horn of oil. The vial anointing is birthed through impatience. It is a result of a child of **GOD** who does not want to wait on **GOD**'s appointed time. **GOD** has set aside great things for us. But because we are consumed with what is going on around us, we want our reward right now. We see everyone around us who appear to be blessed and prosperous. But we fail to realize that it is, in fact, the waiting and the patience which actually makes our reward great. Israel's impatience caused them to seek something that they saw everyone else with, a physical king. They became unsatisfied with their Heavenly **KING** who was always around and never failed them. They looked to man as their source not realizing that man will sometimes disappoint. This caused them to desire a fleshly king, one that they could see and touch. And to add insult to **GOD**, they told <u>Samuel</u> to make them a king. They did not ask **GOD** to make them a king. The peasant must understand that if he/she are to become a true king/queen, then they must never allow man to <u>make</u> them ANYTHING. That is solely **GOD**'s decision.

1Samuel 8:4-5
4 Then all the elders of Israel gathered themselves together, and came to Samuel unto Ramah,

5 And said unto him, Behold, thou art old, and thy sons walk not in thy ways: now make us a king to judge us like all the nations.

Though it was not pleasing to **GOD**, **HE** gave them what they <u>thought</u> they wanted. But it was the opposite of **HIS** desire for them.

1 Samuel 8:6-22
6 But the thing displeased Samuel, when they said, Give us a king to judge us. And Samuel

prayed unto the LORD.

7 And the LORD said unto Samuel, Hearken unto the voice of the people in all that they say unto thee: for they have not rejected thee, but they have rejected me, that I should not reign over them.

8 According to all the works which they have done since the day that I brought them up out of Egypt even unto this day, wherewith they have forsaken me, and served other gods, so do they also unto thee.

9 Now therefore hearken unto their voice: howbeit yet protest solemnly unto them, and shew them the manner of the king that shall reign over them.

10 And Samuel told all the words of the LORD unto the people that asked of him a king.

11 And he said, This will be the manner of the king that shall reign over you: He will take your sons, and appoint them for himself, for his chariots, and to be his horsemen; and some shall run before his chariots.

12 And he will appoint him captains over thousands, and captains over fifties; and will set them to ear his ground, and to reap his harvest, and to make his instruments of war, and instruments of his chariots.

13 And he will take your daughters to be confectionaries, and to be cooks, and to be bakers.

14 And he will take your fields, and your vineyards, and your oliveyards, even the best of them, and give them to his servants.

15 And he will take the tenth of your seed, and of your vineyards, and give to his officers, and to his servants.

16 And he will take your menservants, and your maidservants, and your goodliest young men, and your asses, and put them to his work.

17 He will take the tenth of your sheep: and ye shall be his servants.

18 And ye shall cry out in that day because of your king which ye shall have chosen you; and the LORD will not hear you in that day

19 Nevertheless the people refused to obey the voice of Samuel; and they said, Nay; but we will have a king over us;

20 That we also may be like all the nations; and that our king may judge us, and go out before us, and fight our battles.

21 And Samuel heard all the words of the people, and he rehearsed them in the ears of the LORD.

22 And the LORD said to Samuel, Hearken unto their voice, and make them a king. And Samuel said unto the men of Israel, Go ye every man unto his city.

GOD's intended king was to be completely different from the king that was birthed through Israel's impatience. But when we don't wait on **GOD**, we settle for less.

Deuteronomy 17:14-20
14 When thou art come unto the land which the LORD thy God giveth thee, and shalt possess it, and shalt dwell therein, and shalt say, I will set a king over me, like as all the nations that are about me;

15 Thou shalt in any wise set him king over thee, whom the LORD thy God shall choose: one from among thy brethren shalt thou set king over thee: thou mayest not set a stranger over thee, which is not thy brother.

16 But he shall not multiply horses to himself, nor cause the people to return to Egypt, to the end that he should multiply horses: forasmuch as the LORD hath said unto you, Ye shall henceforth return no more that way.

17 Neither shall he multiply wives to himself, that his heart turn not away: neither shall he greatly multiply to himself silver and gold.

18 And it shall be, when he sitteth upon the throne of his kingdom, that he shall write him a copy of this law in a book out of that which is before the priests the Levites:

19 And it shall be with him, and he shall read therein all the days of his life: that he may learn to fear the LORD his God, to keep all the words of this law and these statutes, to do them:

20 That his heart be not lifted up above his brethren, and that he turn not aside from the commandment, to the right hand, or to the left: to the end that he may prolong his days in his kingdom, he, and his children, in the midst of Israel.

The king that **GOD** <u>allowed</u> Israel to have was a man by the name of Saul. Saul was chosen to be Israel's first king. He did not have all of the qualifications, but he looked the part.

1 Samuel 9:1-2
1 Now there was a man of Benjamin, whose name was Kish, the son of Abiel, the son of Zeror, the son of Bechorath, the son of Aphiah, a Benjamite, a mighty man of power.

2 And he had a son, whose name was Saul, a choice young man, and a goodly: and there was not among the children of Israel a goodlier person than he: from his shoulders and upward he was higher than any of the people.

GOD told Samuel that Saul was the man that **HE** had chosen for the current task.

1 Samuel 9:15-17
15 Now the LORD had told Samuel in his ear a day before Saul came, saying,

16 To morrow about this time I will send thee a man out of the land of Benjamin, and thou shalt anoint him to be captain over my people Israel, that he may save my people out of the hand of the Philistines: for I have looked upon my people, because their cry is come unto me.

17 And when Samuel saw Saul, the LORD said unto him, Behold the man whom I spake to thee of! this same shall reign over my people.

Saul is the example of the vial anointing.

1Samuel 10:1
1 Then Samuel took a vial of oil, and poured it upon his head, and kissed him, and said, Is it not because the LORD hath anointed thee to be captain over his inheritance?

Vial, in Hebrew, means to pour but to run out.
(Refer to The New Strong's Exhaustive Concordance of the

Bible)

The vial anointing is a temporary anointing and will eventually run out. By settling for the vial anointing, the peasant will miss tremendous blessings. They will forfeit the glory that they would have eventually experienced if they had just waited on their time to rule. But by not waiting on their time, they miss key processing and make grave mistakes that will cause them to disobey **GOD**, and lose what they thought they would always have. As stated in chapter one, Saul was rejected by **GOD** due to disobedience and the crown was given to **GOD's** first pick, David.

1 Samuel 13:9-14

9 *And Saul said, Bring hither a burnt offering to me, and peace offerings. And he offered the burnt offering.*

10 *And it came to pass, that as soon as he had made an end of offering the burnt offering, behold, Samuel came; and Saul went out to meet him, that he might salute him.*

11 *And Samuel said, What hast thou done? And Saul said, Because I saw that the people were scattered from me, and that thou camest not within the days appointed, and that the Philistines gathered themselves together at Michmash;*

12 *Therefore said I, The*

Philistines will come down now upon me to Gilgal, and I have not made supplication unto the Lord: I forced myself therefore, and offered a burnt offering.

13 And Samuel said to Saul, Thou hast done foolishly: thou hast not kept the commandment of the Lord thy God, which he commanded thee: for now would the Lord have established thy kingdom upon Israel for ever.

14 But now thy kingdom shall not continue: the Lord hath sought him a man after his own heart, and the Lord hath commanded him to be captain over his people, because thou hast not kept that which the Lord commanded thee.

David is the perfect example of the horn anointing. The horn symbolizes a peak of a mountain, a ray of light and power.
(Refer to The New Strong's Exhaustive Concordance of the Bible)

David was to be that ray of light unto Israel. The king that **GOD** had in mind for **HIS** people. One that would rule with power and authority given to him by **GOD HIMSELF**. And not only that, but he would have the mind and the heart to seek **GOD** and follow **HIS** commands. He would do this realizing that he would always have a need for **GOD** because he was not perfect and was not without faults. If the peasant ever wants to reach his/her designated mountain top, then he/she must wait on the anointing of the horn. The anointing of the horn takes much process. David went through many trials, storms, and battles before he could take his thrown. And his legacy was not cut off as Saul's was. It was passed down from generation to generation. And it was through his seed that **GOD** gave us our Savior, **JESUS CHRIST**. The peasant must wait on the horn anointing so that not only he/she reigns, but the royal mantle is passed down to their children for generations to come.

Chapter 10
"Awake"

Psalm 57:7-11
7 My heart is fixed, O God, my heart is fixed: I will sing and give praise.

8 Awake up, my glory; awake, psaltery and harp: I myself will awake early.

9 I will praise thee, O Lord, among the people: I will sing unto thee among the nations.

10 For thy mercy is great unto the heavens, and thy truth unto the clouds.

11 Be thou exalted, O God, above the heavens: let thy glory be above all the earth.

What I've found in this day in time is that there are some things that we as believers have gotten away from or are missing concerning giving **GOD** a proper praise.

Psalm 57:8
8 Awake up, my glory; awake, psaltery and harp: I myself will awake early.

Glory here is defined as our tongue.
(Refer to The New Strong's Exhaustive Concordance of the Bible)

David, when on the run from king Saul, prayed many prayers of distress. But he made up in his mind that in spite of all that he was experiencing, he would muster a proper praise to offer unto **GOD**. "Awake up, my glory". Here David is simply saying awake up my tongue, my voice, my praise. What I'm noticing is that believers, the body of **CHRIST**, the church, is losing it's voice, it's tongue, it's praise. I'm not implying that we've lost it totally. But we've lost the type of praise that will cause **GOD** to react quickly. We've lost the type of praise that pleases **HIM**. We send up praises, but now they are watered down and mediocre. They are not full of zeal, energy, and fire as they once were. This is because our adversary, the devil, wants us to believe that **GOD** won't perform what **HE** promised in our lives. But this is one of his many lies and the peasant must never believe it.

Numbers 23:19
19 God is not a man, that he should lie; neither the son of man, that he should repent: hath he said, and shall he not do it? or hath he spoken, and shall he not make it good?

The peasant must never lose his/her tongue in any season that they are in. David is speaking to himself and telling his tongue to wake up. He realizes that in order for him to obtain the grace (the divine assistance) to make it through his tough seasons, then he would have to give **GOD** the right kind of praise. The same principle must apply to the peasant. We must never allow our test and trials, or should I say, our training effect our praises unto our **KING** of kings. The peasant must never forget that.

Psalm 34:1
1 I will bless the Lord at all times: his praise shall continually be in my mouth.

Psalm 103:1
1 Bless. The Lord, O my soul: and all that is within me, bless his holy name.

Psalm 103:22

22 Bless the Lord, all his works in all places of his dominion: bless the Lord, O my soul.

This is the right kind of praise. The more you give **GOD** the proper praise, the more **HE** will want to do for you because this tells **HIM** that you are willing to obey and give **HIM** what **HE** wants and not what you feel like giving **HIM**. The peasant will not always feel like giving **GOD** praise. But if we praise **GOD** based on how we feel, then a lot of times we will miss the mark and rob **HIM** of what **HE** deserves. Thus the king/queen will go lacking a key quality of their royal make up. So the peasant must praise **GOD,** by faith and not by feeling, so that he/she can grow into the king/queen that they are to become.

Chapter 11
You Are Closer Than You Think

2 Samuel 2:1-4
1 And it came to pass after this, that David enquired of the Lord, saying, Shall I go up into any of the cities of Judah? And the Lord said unto him, Go up. And David said, Whither shall I go up? And he said, Unto Hebron.

2 So David went up thither, and his two wives also, Ahinoam the Jezreelitess, and Abigail Nabal's wife the Carmelite.

3 And his men that were with him

did David bring up, every man with his household: and they dwelt in the cities of Hebron.

4 And the men of Judah came, and there they anointed David king over the house of Judah. And they told David, saying, That the men of Jabeshgilead were they that buried Saul.

Here, David has just learned that the man that was trying to kill him, king Saul, was dead. And now the manifestation of **GOD's** promise for his life is starting to unfold. So David, the man after **GOD's** own heart, seeks the **LORD** for direction as to where to go from here. Even though the peasant begins to see **GOD's** hand moving, he/she must never eliminate **GOD** from any equation. We must allow **HIM** to lead us from start to finish. As stated in the previous chapter, praise is key. GOD directs David right to praise. David must go to Judah, which means praise. But David is wise enough to know that even though Judah is a place of praise, he must still seek **GOD** for the correct place in Judah to go. Sometimes we could be doing the right things but not exactly the way that **GOD** wants us to. In this particular case, **GOD** directs David to a city in Judah called Hebron.

Hebron - seat of association. It is also defined as company, a spell, charmer, and enchantment.
(Refer to The New Strong's

Exhaustive Concordance of the Bible)

The peasant must be very careful to surround his or herself with the right people. When you are about to be crowned, Hebron can make you or break you. The peasant must be careful of the company he/she keeps. For some desire **GOD's** will for your life and want to crown you king. But Satan will use others to try to charm you and cast a spell on you to keep you from walking in the door of your palace, the door that you are standing right in front of. They will come with subtle conversation and false praises and prophecies. Pretending to be with you but in fact they are very much against you.

Matthew 7:15
Beware of false prophets, which come to you in sheep's clothing, but inwardly they are ravening wolves.

You have now become too close for comfort for the devil and he must now do everything he can to stop you. These attacks may come in various ways. It may come through your spouse, your children, your finances, your church, your job, other loved ones, or all of the above. This is why, again, the right kind of praise is important. In *2 Samuel 2:4*, the men of Judah came and anointed David to be King over the house of Judah. But this is not David's final destination. **GOD's** promise is that David would be king over ALL of Israel. The peasant must never settle for part of the promise. He/she must go through all of the process in order for them to walk in their promise in it's totality. Like David, before the peasant can be king over their promise, they must be king over their praise.

Chapter 12
"All Hail The King"

2 Samuel 5:3
3 So all the elders of Israel came to the king to Hebron; and king David made a league with them in Hebron before the LORD: and they anointed David king over Israel.

Finally, the hour is at hand. This peasant boy, now a mighty man, has reached his defining moment. All that he has gone through has prepared him for now and for that which is to come. He has endured rejection, depression, low self-esteem, attacks, pursuits, wars (physically, mentally, and spiritually), disappointment sadness, hurt, and shame. And he has overcome them all. He has learned how to keep **GOD** first. How to keep himself encouraged, and how to master his praise. He has developed a winner's and a fighter's mentality when his circumstances warranted him to give up and quit. He is a leader of both the small and the great. But a follower of the **GREATEST**. His rule shall not be with firm authority alone, but with love, compassion, wisdom, humility and mercy. He is a king but yet a servant. His heart is to please the **LORD**. He is not defined by where he came from, but where **GOD** called him to. If you would notice in *2 Samuel 5:3*, David did not go and get the crown of Israel. But because he pleased **GOD** so much, the crown came to him. To the reader of this book, you **are** how **GOD** sees you. You are no longer peasants, but kings/queens. The poor, lowly farmer is now royalty. Rejoice for the **LORD** is here, your coronation is at hand.

Psalm 34:6
6 This poor man cried, and the LORD heard him, and saved him out of all his troubles.

The grace of GOD be upon you to rule well, Your Highness.

"ALL HAIL THE KING."

www.ingramcontent.com/pod-product-compliance
Lightning Source LLC
Chambersburg PA
CBHW071143090426
42736CB00012B/2202